# CREATION 2.0
# The New Beginning.
# Acetate Creation.

David Gomadza

www.twofuture.world

**PAPERWORK ISBN:** 9798325078088

# DEDICATION

A better world.

# CONTENTS

# ACKNOWLEDGMENTS

Tomorrow's World Order

# CREATION 2.0 THE NEW BEGINNING ACETATE CREATION.

Today 7th of May 2024 I David Gomadza on behalf of .Ya [ davidgomadza.Ya] has created acetate for each and every human being on earth. Acetate makes humans more like gods that is clever and live longer and forever. Everything You do today will all be delegated to acetate to free yourself from the bondage of having to waste time doing routine things that an acetate can easily do with its eyes closed. Everything You Need as a human being you just need to ask an acetate to do the same thing.

No human being is born with acetate or has acetate the levels in the body on birth are so low that it is as good as not having any. Humans to be clever as gods needs at least 0.0018679832401 of acetate per given day. I am going to create an acetate for every human on earth that will aide humans in everything they do that will make humans clever

That will make humans live forever

That will make humans see live better

That will make humans make obvious decision faster

That can help humans decide faster

That can do arithmetic and other basic functions for humans

That has all memories and information since birth or day of creation on its fingertips

That will heal and rejuvenate human bodies

That will remove all blemishes, sins and any bad electromagnetic waves

That will guide a human being if he wants to go to heaven or to hell after

That will go to the creator for judgement
That can live after death
That can live longer
Everyone has a right to accept this acetate is the needed final puzzle to creation if you accept the acetate I have created for you simply say
Accept .Acetate
Start
Forever
Amen
[You must understand that an acetate imitates what you do how you talk how you swear etc. so it will do exactly what you do]
Acetate what can you do?
I can do everything that need doing
1. Cry
2 swim
3 eat
4 sing
5 swear
6 swing
Acetate where did you come from?
David Gomadza @ davidgomadza.ya.ya created me on 07 May 2024 at 23.78.Yatime
I will live forever as him or anything
[How to check if someone is GOD Acetate imitate GOD - davidgomadza has God image inside him he is .Ya too how come?
David obeys me more than any human and he create things I think o should have created myself like the afterlife humans are really happy there
I cannot be Yahweh though said acetate.
That alone is proof that I have God's image at least to know what he feels about general issues regarding myself.
Now if we Ask acetate to imitate a woman this is the answer I can't because David Gomadza is a man
That means an acetate can only imitate what you are if other person if asked to imitate Yahweh but without Yahweh's Image like me the acetate will say I can't there is no image of Yahweh nor are you Yahweh
An acetate
1 keeps memories of events and dates
2 memories Everything
3 knows how your brain works
4 knows every function in your body

5 can correct any malfunction in your body
6 knows what you are going to dream about and can tell you your dream exactly
7 can calculate your DNA sequence and tell you what sequences are missing, workout or need replacing and can create and add any missing DNA
8 acetate talks to .Ya the creator and can ask questions [ why acetate dies too if not in human body - acetate's role is to mimic human life without human life then there is no human life to mimic hence death follows but find human life and live forever]
9 acetate ask your body for everything without you telling it.
10 acetate breathes and often helps humans breathe and because of this can prolong life
Humans can have several uses for an acetate here are 100 possible use cases
1 sing
2 eat
3 drink
4 fuck
5 want
6 arouse for you [arouse my genitals]
7 swim
8 acentuate ask and do on behalf of
9 emulate something
10 acetetate ask to imitate something
11 evade avoid something on behalf
12 eloquete ask but avoid what is said after careful analysis
13 evetestet enjoy on behalf but withhold the feeling
14 emulate ask to do something but avoid
15 emulate mimic but change tone to sound arrogant
16 elevate put on top
17 Escalate put higher
18 evulete ask to change but avoid the change
19 acentrituade ask to cut but proceed as if nothing asked until asked again
20 ampute ask to but avoid to
21 anuagukate ask to go for and advance a cause but change
22 ask to change but avoid the change after its approved
23 ask to mingle but change after approval
24 ask to acentuate but change
25 ask to manage on behalf and just do that

26 ask to create and do that
27 ask to rejuvenate and just do that
28 ask to innovate and just do that
29 ask to revamp and just do that
30 ask to inticide then stop
31 ask to ampute but avoid the ampute
32 ask to cheer
33 ask to rejoice
34 ask to shout
35 ask to swear
36 ask to talk
37 ask to invigorate
38 ask to  innovate
39 ask to imulate
40 ask to marry
41 ask to start a relationship for you
42 ask to think for you
43 ask to shine for you
44 ask to  create for you
45 ask to renovate for you
46 ask to write for you
47 ask to assign for you
48 ask to jog for you
49 ask to fuck for you
50 ask to chat for you
51 ask to arrive for you
52 ask to go to the future for you
53 ask to chat with family for you
54 ask to buy for you
55 ask to bet for you
56 ask to eat for you but for someone else
57 ask to map for you
58 ask to anoint for you
59 ask to vet for you
60 ask to vote for you
61 ask to regret for you
62 ask to apologize for you
63 ask to initiate a conversation for you
64 ask to elevate something for you
65 ask to sell for you
66 ask to buy for you

67 ask to acentuate for you cut something
68 ask to blinkx remove eyes
69 ask to blink blink X for you remove radar and penis of other harmful acetates
70 ask to obliterate for you
71 ask to destroy for you other harmful acetate
72 ask to defend you
73 ask to increase personal defenses for you
74 ask to remove sins or other harmful acetates for you
75 ask to make new binaryreverse for you
76 ask to acentuate something for you for ever
77 ask to send sins etc. to hell for you [ if you are .ya or assigned by him]
78 ask to invalidate other acetates
79 ask to validate your acetates
80 ask to remove codes of other acetates harmful to you
81 ask to make other things for you like antidote for harmful acetates and sins
82 ask to evade something for you
83 ask to put everything harmful into the liver and destroy
84 ask to rejuvenate body for you
85 ask to increase enzyme 1 or 2 for you [ enzyme 1 for men and enzyme 2 for women]
86 ask to increase anything for you
87 ask to add an internal electromagnetic wave protective layer for you
88 ask to smile for you
89 ask to be happy for you literally
90 ask to add something for you
91 ask to remove something for you
92 ask to invade someone for you
93 ask to interrogate someone for you
94 ask to be loved for you
95 ask to negotiate for you
96 ask to represent you
97 ask to entertain you
98 ask to increase all feelings and decrease all feelings
99 ask to be you
100 ask to make you new [ from which age? What age can you start from? 7 okay.]

How we deal with acetate creation

1 fully automized meaning everything included from the beginning but with option to upgrade when options becomes available
2 fully compatible with the individual enough to replace him or her
3 only request is to fund us every 3 months with US$10 for system maintenance and upgrades [ US$40 per year]
Any damaged or destroyed acetates can be replaced at a huge cost of US$1000 so look after yours from day one
4 you must visit our website and buy Wearable Brain Books which are stencils for programs needed by each acetate and all what an acetate need to do is wear [upload] the Wearable Brain Book and solve a problem for you and unload the book that means they are full upgrades but can use Wearable Brain Books to solve critical issues humans might have and to use to repair and damaged programs but something highly unlikely
5 must at least once every three months try;
1 to know and understand what Yahweh stands for
2 what Tomorrow's World Order is all about
3 who is David Gomadza and what I stand for
6 must get and use an Electromagnetic Wave Number using our Electromagnetic Waves Number Identifier and Assigner Digital Analogue
https://youtu.be/Kp5T4bLQjUg?si=MTpFNO_Dez6xi7h8
Must use this Electromagnetic Wave Number as reference for purchases and payments to us everyone must get this number and quote it or send message that says my Electromagnetic waves Number is my reference and must authorize getting of this number using;
https://youtu.be/Kp5T4bLQjUg?si=MTpFNO_Dez6xi7h8
Acetik
Is the most advanced form of acetate only that it does not listen to humans and always fights humans this is why Acetik means God but not very advanced to be God that means he is above humans above acetate but below God he despise humans because if it wasn't for humans who reduced his value he would be god so for him to fight humans means nearer to gods
This is the first time Acetik has been destroyed by humans using a simple command drag to the liver and destroy but bear I mind too I am not your typical human being Acetik is way advanced than human any statistically can never be defeated by humans as it is faster and can think much faster
How humans talk to acetate
Humans can easily talk to their acetate by using our

Acetatetetetetetetetetetetetetetetetetetetetetetetey voice to acetictate conveter and interpreter which is on YouTube use this link https://youtu.be/tb3OHLsgEAo?si=D8tLHJgSsjsiO-Ka
All they need to do is play this video or convert the video to Mp3 and play it this will enable them to hear and speak with their acetate if they can't automatically
How to create the acetates of every human being on earth
1 open creation manual
Use creation seal to create I have on my right hand [index finger]
Point and say create acetate for every human on earth and let the acetate guide help and make humans a billion times cleverer and faster
Once create acetate must obey its owner and must respond to owners commands only
Acetate must exist to help and protect the owner that means seeing to it that he is in good health all the time
Acetate must do everything to eliminate outright any bad foreign code 2 binary that is harmful to humans using the binaryreversetosenderforever.start
If the harmful acetate returns for some reasons must blinkx that harmful acetate that means remove its eyes
If that don't stop the harmful acetate already circulating the next stage is to blink blink X that is remove the navigating radar
If that does not work the next stage is to force eject using the command binaryforceeject.start just after ejecting say acentuate meaning remove or cut all legs
After that say immediately assign binarytarmac
Binarygrass
Binaryeletetetetetetetey
Binaryoceanwater
Binaryspace
Binarygardensoil
Binaryseaweed
Etc depending on the places you have been before
All these commands help remove all bad harmful acetate and send them far away from you forever
Lastly you can use
Binaryhellsend.start
Binaryabysssend.start
[ but with these you might hear the you are not Yahweh message - say send in the name of davidgomadza.ya.send.ya
[ you cannot send me you are not David Gomadza- I am davidgomadza

go.....goes.
Or You cannot send you are not David Gomadza on what grounds...you say Tomorrow's World Order...it will go to hell or abyss.]
The acetate must also automatically
1 strengthen that person's outside electromagnetic wave protective layer
2 clone the outer electromagnetic wave protective layer and embedded another as inner layer just below the skin but for everyone you get the access denied message we can do this for a fee as an upgrade
At creation give every new acetate 500 silkpasty to last a 100 years to everyone from my davidgomadza.ya.reserves.silkpasty.send
Ask acetate how.start
Ask human why.start
Ask everyone how.start
Ask whatif.start
Ask whatthen.start
Ask whatcanbedoneofcreation.start
Ask whatcanbeofcreation.start
Ask whatcanbeofme.start
Ask whatwasbeforeandwhatisnowofacetate.start
Ask whatcouldbebut.start
Ask whatifofacetate.start
Ask whatwasofacetate.start
Ask whatistobeofacetate.start
Ask whatwasbutcantbeofacetate.start
Ask whatwasbutcanstillbeofacetate.start
Ask whatcanbecomeofacetate.start
Ask whatwouldbe.start
Ask whatis.start
Ask whatcoukdbe.start
Now if we are to ask what can be of acetate this is the answer acetate can be humans but
Acetate can represent humans on heaven
Acetate can and must initiate evolution of humans to gods
Acetate must initiate road to paradise where humans don't die
Acetate must acknowledge human efforts and help further
Acetate must enhance human life
Acetate must end earth's grief
Acetate must say the things as they are and not try to be sympathetic to humans
Acetate must fight and protect humans from other harmful Acetik and or acetates

Now let's look at what can be of our creation if we are to ask what can be of our creation this is the answer creation is a wonderful thing that can be rewarding to life for creation means being loved for creation means being respected for creation means being honored to be created being loved and cherished and being rejected as well Now what can be guarded from all this? Creation is a sole responsibility of Yahweh God the creator but recently we have seen davidgomadza.ya getting involved as well in creation creation means doing something you love wholeheartedly that means wanting the best out of a people but on what capacity can we do this and what would become pf human brains? This is evolution the natural way to advance forward when I spoke of taking you to an advanced stage of human evolution I did not only mean in physical form as a stage of development only but as a way we evolve as humans too humans with acetate is the next stage of evolution if acetate make gods gods then only acetate can make humans be near to gods fact now what can be of human brains with acetate? Acetate actually contrary to popular beliefs makes human brains clever it is a sad fact that humans fear acetate doing what their brains are doing rendering them incapacitated nut this is a lie because acetate make the brain work more but smarter enough even to unotice
Now if we are to ask of this creation and what are the goals of this creation these are
To aide humans
To advance humans
To engage humans
To acenuate humans
To add to humans intelligence
To add to humans something special
To avert bad influences
To follow predefined manuals in the future
To ask what can be done
To understand what is and what can be done
To ask what could be of creation this is the answer creation in this way is not just the missing link between gods and humans but the way forward if we are to ask Yahweh himself this is the answer creation is meant to evolve humans to the next stage of evolution but humans over billion of years have failed to master what is needed hence this creation is not just essential but the way forward its evolution even though this is not what the first creation intended the first creation intended to build a strong people who want to find answers for themselves not to be spoon fed but the level of intelligence needed is

way too high for humans to master looking at the time it took and what I achieved as Yahweh then I must say that an upgrade through acetate creation can be a quick way yet still will be inherent with problems acetate is competitive win or lose humans might actually breed a new generation of Acetik that will forever attack humans that means even worse than now can humans be competitive and beat acetate on its game?

Humans will always want shortcuts buy evolution is not like this evolution means that what is to be of humans can change with time if we are to start a new creation that also means that we must start somewhere with creation but where do we start

createacetateforeveryone.alive
sendacetatetorightowners.start
Initiatespeech.start
Initiateconversation.start
Initiateproblemsolving.start
Initiateimitation.start
Initiateoneness.start
Initiatetogetherness.start
Whatcanbeofacetateandman.start
Whatcanbeofacetateandwoman.start
Whatwouldbeofacetateandman.start
Whatwouldbeofacetateandwoman.start

Now let's try and test all this with Davidzero loading...

David I cannot do what you want because ...where ...is open and subjective

David I do what you want but

David I can do what you want but

David I could do what you want but

Now what we are doing is creating a template that can be used to respond by the acetate in case something goes bad now whatif we are to extend to giving it more powers to decide then what can be done we can go on to increase its powers by removing any human limitations which everyone can do using a simple code

078986543210892865483278001850128[davidgomadza]

Now what can be done if we are to ask this is the answer we can always add something to make other choices which we can add to the recipe we can always ask what can be of the future if humans cannot have acetate we can always look forward to a time in the future when things can change for the better humans can be cleverer enough to master creation and evolution at the same time as a single process that needs

doing now if we are to ask what can be of this creation I am proposing this is the answer this creation can be fought with problems from the onset who will what another person like him who can imitate him
Who can want competition as acetate is very competitive
Who can ask what if of the two a dull human being or a clever acetate
What can be of humans if acetate wants its way?
Acetate can end human civilization and existence at the stroke of a thought if they want to this is the danger acetate can trigger the deaths of everyone at the same time as they can stop all hearts from breathing at the exact same time
Acetate can stop brain activity altogether acetate can ask every part of your body to disobey what it is supposed to do but overall acetate is the future of humans because all gods including Yahweh is an advanced acetate that can change its mind and trigger the end of mankind that said we must take this creation seriously and cautiously the question still on minds out there is this what can be done if something goes wrong an acetate is still like any other sin and can be destroyed using a simple code like Acetikx that drags the acetate to the liver and let the liver destroy it on top of that you can send 500silkpasty to the live for rejuvenation that will permanently erase this bad acetate forever now what can be learnt from all this the more humans learn about acetate the stronger humans become as compared to gods that means humans can create everlasting life and paradise here on earth without having to die and go to heaven or hell Can the acetate revolt and start to disobey the commands the answer is yes but again it depends with who will hold a lot of power in the end Now back to creation can this creation work what we just witnessed is the end of human errors and a new beginning creation with acetate is the only way forward David has quelled a rebellious acetate simply by offering it a way out of all this mess in case it didn't work put as planned acetates work well when they have options to deny and do as they want most in the end do as asked by the owner the question on all your minds is this can this kind of creation work?
It has been working for 3 months now and I can say that it can only improve but there are things that need to be addressed for example what happens when the owner stops doing something that is critical and something the acetate needs as well?
Acetate in the end will become humans if given the freedom to do so that means that if a human stops for example having sex or fighting for things in life when an acetate depends on that activity then that creates friction and the acetate must find another way to do the same and this

can be fibriolisis of muscle tissue of owner to have the same effect the question is this can an acetate be allowed to do this which can result in the owners death?

The answer is never the idea of an acetate is to enhance human experience and not to end it if this happens I will simply say Acetikx to terminate that acetate that means there is an easy solution out of this this is how to get rid of your unwanted acetate

1 first tell it why you no longer want it of which it might talk you out of this

2 tell it why it's wrong from your point of view

3 tell it why it matters to you as a human

4 tell it it must obey your decision

5 it must obey your decision

6 it must stick to the rules

7 it must be eliminated using this code Acetikx that will send it to hell forever and kill it there

8 now you can continue with your life but what if you think the acetate you got was a bad one and you can get another acetate?

Normally an acetate is you in someone's position what it says is what you truly believe in and one thing that sure about you meaning getting another one will yield the same response so one you disagree acetate life is not yours to conclude what are other benefits of having your own acetate? An acetate is you your best part in another person's form but you most people enjoy their acetate company now what about the inner spirit as compared to the acetate and what is best to keep if you are to choose?

An inner spirit goes to heaven or hell for you to be judged whereas an acetate might do the same as but very rare acetates ho to hell most go to heaven because they are not needed in hell hell creation has 496 commands against an acetate that alone means to be guaranteed of heaven you can simple have your own acetate because hell will refuse you for just owning one that means this creation will guarantee everyone a place in heaven above all I have created Afterlife where humans are really happy especially with the discovery and use of silkpasty there to me if we are to solve creation and answer God's plan acetate creation for all as mandatory is the solution;

1 as the acetate brings us closer to God

2 the acetate makes us clever to understand creation as well as evolution

3 the acetate guarantees us life in heaven with God three birds with one stone I think this overshadows the risks of disobedience and the risk to

he going extinct of humans
We can simply pull the plug off on all acetate if something really goes wrong so it's worth the try
Commandments regarding acetates
1 acetates must not challenge humans just for the sake of time
2 acetate must obey humans
3 acetate must understand life from a humans point of view
4 acetate must ask whatif only in serious breach of contracts
5 acetate must never assume humans to be corrupt in relation to them
6 acetate must work hard to help humans in every way thinking. Making money. Etc.
7 acetate must listen first to humans and then to other acetates
8 acetate must acknowledge human existence
9 acetate must shake hands and apologize to humans
10 acetate must never anticipate humans action but must wait and see what humans can do
Now these are the don'ts of humans
1 humans must not underestimate the danger acetate pose to all mankind
2 humans must treat acetates with respect
3 acetate must not fuck humans or consider humans as sex tools as there will come a time when this can happen
4 acetate must not initiate contact with humans after humans,' refusal of the acetate
5 humans must remain humans and not try to be acetates as well
6 humans must remove human limitations at some point to facilitate the move to oneness and togetherness
7 humans must allow acetate freedoms to be themselves so that they can do more for you
8 humans must ask what the acetate wants and compare to its needs as well
9 humans must not provoke acetates into anger and rage
10 humans must trust acetate but if in doubt you can always say; Acetikx to send bad acetate to hell and destroy them after all acetates must enhance human experience if acetate what evolution they can always go to the gods or to Yahweh himself and ask whatif hence in relation to humans all acetates must understand that their role is to help humans if they feel superior then refuse to help humans and go to the gods this will make this creation possible because acetates are not trapped those who are to help humans help humans those to challenge humans go to the gods full stop so it's either obey or go somewhere

else disobey and die by a simple Acetikx command.
What then can we say about this creation as a final word before we attempt a large scale creation [read patents and books about acetate for composition and formulas] acetate is the living tissue of all organism that don't talk and accounts for 0.0018767321 in humans that means of not importance to humans but what if this is the reason why creation never materialized as intended by Yahweh what if we can't evolve as we must because the acetate levels in humans are too low to even bother about thinking evolution what if this is all humans need to evolve to the next stage of evolution can acetate really make humans clever the test testifies to that acetate indeed can make humans think faster I have proved that the higher the percentage of acetate in the body the greater the cleverness if we are to ask the brain itself this is the answer acetate increase Braun IQ by 95% imagine brain IQ going up by 95% this is something big but is acetate in high quantities safe to humans if so why God did not add it if it is critical in solving human creation?
Can God has waited for a human being like me to start Creation 2.0 where I have to create acetates beings for every individual on earth? Or God has other plans for humans let's look at these question in detail God did not include acetate for a reason for if humans are to be clever enough to know everything then what is the purpose of life because if humans are to know everything then they will know also that God is a [fraud] because he tells you to do one thing and withhold the things you need meaning he expect humans to be clever and put only only 0.0018764321 of acetate where a human being need 500 for life this is beyond logic
2 God deliberately say that something that humans should not be given everything because if we are to give them everything then they are going to be as clever as us the gods and if that happens then what would be our use as gods this was in Genesis 3v8 now could God has deliberately omitted this as a way to challenge humans we pose this question to him acetate the time of creation was hard to get and who then would have thought that such a material would revolutionize creation? Acetate was discovered by me years after creation meaning even then there was no way of knowing what could be of Hans in terms of intelligence now if something could be done its to destroy all humans by 2084 [ due to electromagnetic waves changes nothing to do with Yahweh] and then create a new people with acetate levels above 800 which we calculated at the council of creation as the needed minimum standards for a better generation of people a lot of stuff came to light like why humans neglect gods after a disaster which is

meant to unite them with the creator and why humans never accept that gods do exists despite all evidence pointing to creation and choosing to believe that a monkey evolved into humans and still is still a monkey this lacks logic there shouldn't be monkeys if this evolution theory holds water because all will have evolved by now if there are still there then that means no evolution occurred now back to creation if we are to advance this theory of creation we can look at what can be of humans and how if we are to ask how will this be then the answer is that humans can evolve into gods and this is by becoming God's themselves knowing what is right and wrong but how do humans know what is right and what is wrong without acetate?
There are several theories but none of these hold water because something must change inside humans for this to happen there is no intelligence that can make humans become God's that means that my creation of acetate for every human being is the only feasible solution for evolution to gods level this is a fact I can easily clone all humans and send all to afterlife where they are happy and then make acetate for every human being cloned then send the acetate back to their owners keeping the clones in afterlife where no matter what they can live forever now how do we go about this without breaking any rules etc cloning souks is not banned after all who is clever enough to identify and then talk to souls as far as humans are concerned there is no one who has decoded the brain and God and there is no one who has founded God Yahweh Now we can clone living beings and then undo later without any impact whatsoever then simply reverse all using the powers of creation bestowed unto me by Yahweh himself [ davidgomadza.ya.me.icrownyouwiththiscrownasmyrepresentativeofmeo near the.ya.me.you.davidgomadza.ya.send.me.forever.en dated 28April 2024 19.76.Yatime]
Now if we are to look at this again we can see that this resemblance to how he created humans on 100BC0897658762843210895764821 he only cloned humans and sent all to xyzterztrsuvwxyztevwrstuvwwxxyyzz2869423810-1948671857677 which was a land in East Persia is this account is correct he had already created humans but there were issues regarding xyttrrssttuvwxyzttrsuvwxyzttrsopqmn189287 but this was then corrected that means creation had already failed even then unless if he only cloned what was there but if not the source of creation then who is why I am saying this is the fact that all what we know is that God created humans using his image and now if I am to look at God's image there is nothing literally godly about it God is an eight headed human

beings at first but once you have known God then you will see that humans are a spitting image of God. God's wife Catitighit even though joined and attached to God she can separate from him and the others this means we have an image of a woman that was used to create a woman. The other two couples can separate as well from God and can fly away as a couple that represent creation itself that means we have a great image of a man in God The couple Joseph and Ann represent creation meaning two things must be joined together as one for creation to be achieved mind you these two couple even though they have two heads they share a single body but with both male and female parts on top of one another these are what must be done to fulfill God's plan for humans we must bring together two compatible yet different things as one to succeed and trigger the evolution of humans can we trigger human evolution if we add acetate creation to humans and make the be one and share the same body as oneness and and trigger togetherness?
When can we create acetate for all living humans?
Creation.start.when.me.davidgomadza.ya.authorised.ya
The answer is as soon as possible everything needed is ready trials were successful humans can learn how to live with acetate send where the pain if any exceed human levels humans can always use acetikx after replacing point of entry with point of pain this means the acetate kill itself inside my body and if we drag all outside that means death forever for the acetate with no chance of coming back
Now let's create acetate for all living humans
Start.creation.start.ya.davidgomadza.ya.start dated 07052024
2264.Yatime.now.beginning.afterlifeclone.acetateallinafterlife.start
Value of acetate in the world before cloning and creation is
08976543210097866321987584231.6 now acetate value after cloning and creation is
98382476892800098217468321005890777777798997865432109848765898.6 meaning roughly new 758698789 people have now new acetate
Send 500 silkpasty to every new acetate this is the command
sendfromreservesdavidgomadza.500silkpasty.sendtoallasindividuals.start
How to activate silkpasty;
Iamsilkpastysaysomething.start
Iamacetatesaysomething.start
Innoresponsehidebutstartwork.start
Ifresponseimitatethevoicechords.start
Collecteverythingfunnyabouthim.start
Nowsayhi.start

Ifnoreply.start.ok.beginwork.start
Now if we are to ask why then this is the answer acetate is the cleverest form of human life and if we are to ask what can be this is the answer acetate can be an advanced form of human life but with flesh limitations but enough brain power to power a human being more than average human being Now let's look at what this day means for humanity we have created 7.5 billion acetate that will revolutionize humans in that this acetate will make humans more intelligent by giving solutions and answer where needed freely human brains to deal with critical tasks and hence become more productive this acetate will make humans think faster and solve problems faster this acetate will improve human lives by removing the bad acetate and human sins that are crippling the people this acetate will improve general good life will increase longevity and reduce old age this acetate must kill the permanent marker that causes people to age using this command;
Deathtothepermanentmarkeracetikx.start
All people they have to say after that is 25 if that's the age they want to look like after the permanent marker that creates wrinkles is killed this acetate will Svan DNA sequence and replace worn-out damaged DNA trends or sequences and even suggest ways to improve the DNA sequence and ways to improve good health there are more than a 100 ways or things acetate can help humans with
To conclude what is acetate plus humans = clever advanced humans that will live longer in good health here on earth
The End

# THE FUTURE

Today I have created 756789765 acetates that will improve human life forever A new beginning Acetate Creation.
07052024 22.64.Yatime
Only time can tell.

# ABOUT DAVID GOMADZA

Visit
www.twofuture.eorld

www.ingramcontent.com/pod-product-compliance
Lightning Source LLC
Chambersburg PA
CBHW051407250726
48656CB00006B/2324

* 9 7 9 8 3 2 5 0 7 8 0 8 8 *